THE LIFE AND WORDS OF
MARTIN LUTHER KING, JR.

Ira Peck

Cover photo *Wide World Photos*

SCHOLASTIC INC.

New York Toronto London Auckland Sydney

12 11 10 9 8 7 6 5 4 3 2   6 7 8 9/8 0 1/9

Printed in the U.S.A.   11

CONTENTS

Black Star

Martin Luther King, Jr., believed in fighting peacefully against evil. Picture of the great Indian leader, Gandhi, hangs on wall.

FOREWORD
"MINE EYES HAVE SEEN THE GLORY"

Early in the evening of April 4, 1968, a rifle bullet ended the life of Martin Luther King, Jr., in Memphis, Tennessee. His death plunged the nation into gloom, just as President John F. Kennedy's death had a few years before.

King was only thirty-nine when he was killed, but he had already been the foremost Negro civil rights leader in the United States for more than twelve years. King became the leader of that movement late in 1955, when he was chosen by Montgomery, Alabama, Negroes to lead a boycott against the city's bus lines. At the time, King was the pastor of a fairly well-to-do Baptist Church in Montgomery. He might have done little more and still led a very useful life. But some people "have greatness thrust upon them," and King was one of these.

When he was elected to lead the boycott, he really didn't want the job. But, once chosen, he felt that he couldn't refuse to serve his people in their cause. King led the Negroes' cause in Montgomery against segregated buses, and overcame every kind of obstacle. Even the danger of violence against himself didn't cause him to flinch. From then on King felt he *had* to lead the Negro people to freedom, not only in Montgomery, but wherever there was racial injustice. When he left his church in Montgomery to return to his home in Atlanta, Georgia, he told his people:

"History has thrust something on me which I cannot turn away."

King never flinched from what he thought was his

duty. Some people said that he went too far, that he was a "troublemaker." Others said that he did not go far enough, that he was, in fact, an "Uncle Tom." King always said that he was a middle-of-the-road man. Some Negroes, he said, wished to do nothing about segregation and injustice, and just let things go on as they were. Others were full of hatred and talked of using violence against white people. His way, non-violence, King said, was the best way — the only way — for the Negro in the United States to win equality and dignity. King warned that if white people did not support his nonviolent movement, many Negroes would turn to "black nationalism" and hatred of all things white. This, he said, would lead to a racial nightmare. The ghetto riots of the summers of 1965-67 seemed to bear him out.

After many attempts on his life, King, the man of nonviolence, finally met a violent death. King knew that he might meet death almost any day after he became a civil rights leader. But at the end he was no longer afraid of dying. The day before he was killed he said:

> It (death) really doesn't matter with me now. Because I have been to the mountaintop. And I've looked over, and I've seen the promised land. I may not get there with you. But I want you to know tonight that we as a people will get to the promised land. So I'm happy tonight. I'm not worried about anything. I'm not fearing any man. Mine eyes have seen the glory of the coming of the Lord!

This, then, is the story of Martin Luther King and his vision.

Police guard the State Capitol in Montgomery, Alabama, in 1965.

UPI

CHAPTER 1
THE MAN AND THE MOMENT

Martin Luther King felt good — real good. He was driving south to Montgomery, Alabama, on a fine, clear, winter day. He was listening to an opera on the car radio. He liked operas, and this one was a favorite. The music was beautiful. So was the country all around him.

But there were even better reasons why King was a happy man this day. He was young (just twenty-five), married, and a minister. What's more, he had his pick of good jobs. Two churches in the North wanted him as a minister. Three colleges had offered him important jobs.

One church in the South had been a little "cagey." It hadn't actually offered him a job as minister. It had just asked him if he would like to preach there some

This movie house in the South had a separate door for "colored."

Sunday. King understood. It would be a kind of test, or trial. If he did well, then he just *might* get the job. It was a good church, and King thought he just *might* want the job.

So here he was, in January, 1954, driving down to Montgomery from his home in Atlanta, Georgia. When King arrived in Montgomery, he looked over the church that had invited him there. It was the Dexter Avenue Baptist Church. A brick building, it had been built soon after the Civil War. From its steps, he could see the beautiful State Capitol building. Jefferson Davis, the President of the Confederacy in the Civil War, had been sworn in there. Montgomery was called "the cradle of the Confederacy."

That night, King began to feel nervous. Would the church members like him? Most of them were educated, intelligent people. Should he try to show them how smart he was? Or should he just depend on the spirit of God to guide him? King liked the second idea better. He said to himself, "Keep Martin Luther King in the background, and God in the foreground, and everything will be all right."

So it was. A month later, the church members

This doctor's office in the South had a "white" sign on door.

asked him to be their minister. Now King had to decide which job to take. He and his wife, Coretta, both resented the South's segregation laws. These laws kept the white and Negro races separated as much as possible. Negroes were kept out of "white" schools, parks, theaters, hotels, and eating places. They had to sit in separate sections in trains and buses. This separation of the races was called "Jim Crow." The aim of Jim Crow was to make Negroes second-class citizens.

In some cases, Jim Crow separation was a custom rather than the law. Negroes and whites went to separate churches, even when they were of the same religion. Negro and white doctors, lawyers, and teachers rarely met together, either.

In the North, King and his wife would not be insulted by Jim Crow laws. Neither would their children, when they had them. King and his wife had both gone to schools in the North. They had been well treated there.

Yet King, with Coretta's consent, decided to take the job in Montgomery, Alabama. The South, they felt, was their home. They had education and training.

It was their duty to try to help less fortunate southern Negroes. Besides, they had a feeling that something wonderful was about to happen in the South. They had a feeling that a new South, free of Jim Crow, was about to be born. Then the South would really grow tall. They wanted to be there to see it happen.

King took over his new job full-time on September 1, 1954. The first few months were a very busy and a very happy time for King. He did the usual things ministers do. He preached on Sundays, married people, and held funeral services. One day a week he visited the sick at home and prayed with them.

But these "usual" duties were not enough for King. He wanted to do more than care for the souls of his church members. He wanted his church to help the sick and the poor. He wanted it to help young people to go to college. He wanted it to help young artists to study. He wanted it to help Negro people to register and vote — a tough job in the South. He wanted it to get Negroes to join the NAACP (National Association for the Advancement of Colored People). The NAACP fought in the courts for the rights of Negroes. King believed that a church that cared only for the souls of its members was "dry as dust." It was the duty of a church to care about the living conditions of people. Because, he said, bad living conditions scar people's souls. Religion, he said, must care about heaven and earth, souls and slums.

The members of King's church liked his unusual ideas. They soon put them into action. In the next few months, more and more people joined the Dexter Avenue Baptist Church. The members gave more and more money for its work. King saw his church grow and was happy. Meanwhile, he was also working on his Ph.D. degree. He would soon be *Dr.* King. These may have been the happiest months of his life.

Then, on December 1, 1955, something happened in Montgomery that changed King's entire life. It also changed the lives of that town's fifty thousand Negro people. Within a few years, it would help change the lives of almost all America's Negro people, and a good many white people, too.

What happened in Montgomery on that day? A Negro woman, Rosa Parks, was seated just behind the "white section" on a bus. By law, whites sat up front, Negroes in the back. Mrs. Parks was going home from her job as a seamstress. Several white people got on the bus. There were no more seats for them in the "white" section. So the bus driver ordered Mrs. Parks, and three other Negroes, to move to the back of the bus. The bus was now full, and Mrs. Parks would have to stand. The three other Negroes obeyed the driver. Mrs. Parks said "No." She would *not* give up her seat. Her feet hurt, she said later.

Why was this so unusual? When Mrs. Parks said "no" to the bus driver, she was breaking the law. The law in Alabama said she had to move to the back of the bus. If she did not obey the driver, she could be arrested and fined — or maybe go to jail. Mrs. Parks was arrested on the spot.

The news of her arrest spread like wildfire among Montgomery's Negroes. They decided to protest. A few days later, they chose Martin Luther King to be their leader. It took him by surprise, but he agreed. Why did they choose King, a new person in their town? Wasn't he, after all, an "outsider"? Perhaps there was something in his life and his beliefs that just made him stand out.

CHAPTER 2
THE MAKING OF A LEADER

Ebony Magazine
Martin Luther King, Sr., fought against the "Jim Crow" system.

Martin Luther King, Jr., was born January 15, 1929, in Atlanta, Georgia. His father was pastor of the Ebenezer Baptist Church there. King, Sr., lived with his family in a large, comfortable house in Atlanta's Negro section. Even during the bad times of the 1930's, the family always had enough to eat and good clothes.

But King, Sr., knew what it was like to be very poor. His father had been a sharecropper, or tenant farmer. He had always owed money to the white landlord. No matter how long, or how hard he worked, he could never get ahead. The family home was a rundown, leaky shack.

King, Sr., did not want that kind of life for himself. At fifteen, he left the farm and went to Atlanta, twenty miles away. He took rough jobs by day, and at night went to school. It took a long time, but he finally got a high school and a college diploma and became a minister. He married the daughter of a leading Atlanta minister and raised a family. His three children were Christine, Martin, Jr., and Alfred Daniel.

Ebony Magazine

Left: The King family lived in this large house in Atlanta, Georgia.
Right: This is Morehouse College in Atlanta, which Martin entered at 15.

King, Sr., hated the South's Jim Crow system. He was a fighter, and his son, Martin, learned some of his first lessons from him. One day, King, Sr., took his young son to a store to buy shoes. They sat down in the first empty seats at the front of the store. A white salesman said to Mr. King politely:

"I'll be glad to wait on you if you'll just move to those seats in the back."

Mr. King said, "There's nothing wrong with these seats. We're very comfortable here."

"I'm sorry," the salesman said. "You'll have to move."

Mr. King became angry. "We'll either buy shoes sitting here," he said, "or we won't buy shoes at all."

Then he took his son by the hand and walked out of the store. "I don't care how long I have to live with this system," he said. "I will never accept it."

Another time Martin was riding with his father in the family car. Mr. King drove past a "Stop" sign by accident. A policeman told him to pull over and said, "All right, boy, let me see your license."

No man likes to be called a "boy." This was just another way of insulting Negroes in the South. Mr. King again got very angry. He pointed to his son and said to the policeman:

"This is a boy. I'm a man. Until you call me one, I will not listen to you."

The policeman couldn't believe any Negro would talk back to him. He was so shocked he wrote out the ticket in a hurry and left.

King, Sr., had won some important victories for his people in Atlanta. He had helped Negro teachers there to get the same pay as white teachers. And he had helped to get rid of Jim Crow (separate for black and white) elevators in the courthouse.

Martin also learned a very important lesson from his mother when he was six. Martin had two young white friends. Their parents ran a store across the street from the Kings' home. Martin and the white boys were always together. Then one day the boys' mother told Martin they could no longer play with him.

Martin didn't understand. He asked his mother about it. His mother took him on her lap and began to explain the South's segregation system. When she finished, she said:

"But don't ever forget this — you are as good as anyone."

It was no wonder that Martin also grew up to hate segregation. As a teenager, he resented sitting in the back of a bus. He felt deeply insulted when he had to sit behind a curtain in a railroad dining car. The whole system, he thought, was both unfair and stupid. Even more, he hated the violence that grew out of segregation. He had seen the Ku Klux Klan riding at night. He had passed places where Negroes had been lynched by mobs. All these things almost made him resent all white people.

In school, Martin was a very bright student. He was especially good at making speeches, and often practiced in front of a mirror. In his last year in high school, he entered a speech contest and won first prize. It was a proud moment in his life.

Because he was smart, Martin skipped two grades in school. He was able to enter Morehouse College, in Atlanta, when he was only fifteen. This was the same college his father had attended. Many other Negro leaders had gone to this school.

At this time, Martin still wasn't sure what he wanted to be. He knew one thing — he wanted to help his people in some way. How could he do it best? Martin wasn't sure. He thought that religion was "out of touch" with the real problems of his people — segregation and poverty. What about being a doctor and healing the sick? For a while Martin thought that might be a good idea. Or should he become a lawyer who would make speeches and defend his people in the courts? He liked that idea best. Yes, he would be a lawyer who would fight for his people's rights in court.

But he soon changed his mind. Two of the leading teachers at Morehouse were ministers. These men showed him that a minister could care about things like segregation, hunger, and sickness. King knew then that he wanted to be a minister. At seventeen, Martin gave a "trial" sermon in his father's church. It made a big hit with the church members. Martin's father got down on his knees and thanked God. At eighteen, Martin became a minister, and his father's assistant.

CHAPTER 3
KING AND GANDHI

Mahatma Gandhi, center, was called "the little brown saint of India" by King. Gandhi led India to freedom using nonviolence.

Martin graduated from Morehouse when he was nineteen. But he felt that he wanted to study even more, so he could become a better minister. In September, 1948, he entered Crozer, a school of religion in Chester, Pennsylvania. The school had one hundred students. Only six were Negroes. Now Martin felt he had to prove what his mother had always told him:

"You are as good as anybody."

Martin studied hard at this time and became an "A" student.

What about his wish to help his people? Martin felt they had two main problems. They were segregated and they were usually poor. He was sure that the two problems went hand in hand. Didn't they usually go to rundown schools? Didn't they always get the "dirty" jobs with the lowest pay? Weren't they always the first to be fired? Yes, he thought, Jim Crow and being poor were really twin evils.

So far, King really hadn't found a way of helping his people. In college he had read a composition by Henry David Thoreau. Thoreau was an American writer who lived more than a hundred years ago. Thoreau believed that a man had the right to disobey any law he thought was evil or unjust. Once he would not pay his taxes as a protest against slavery. He was put in jail. A friend came to visit Thoreau in jail.

"Why are you in jail?" the friend asked him.

"Why are you out of jail?" Thoreau answered.

King liked Thoreau's idea — that men should not obey evil or unjust laws. He read the composition over and over again.

When he entered Crozer, he began to search harder for a way to fight against evil. He read books by the great thinkers and writers. He knew that many people thought that communism was the answer to poverty. But King was against communism. He was against it because it had no place for God. It also took away a man's freedom. And Communists believed that, to win power, they could lie, use force, or even murder people. King was against all those things. There must be a better way than communism, he thought.

Then one day he heard a speech about the great leader of India, Mahatma Gandhi. Gandhi was the "father of his country." After many years, he had in 1947 won freedom for his country from British rule. He had done it in a very unusual way. From the start, he told his people not to use violence against the British. He told them to resist the British by peaceful means only. What peaceful means could they use? They could march. They could sit down or lie down in the streets. They could strike. They could fast. They could boycott British goods.

Gandhi had also read Thoreau's composition. He, too, believed that men had the right to disobey unjust laws. Like Thoreau, he believed that men should gladly go to jail when they break such laws. "Fill the jails," Gandhi said.

But — never use violence. Violence defeats itself. It only brings about more hate and more violence. Gandhi told his followers to meet body force with soul force. He told them to meet hate with love. He told them they must learn to suffer if they wanted to win their freedom. "Rivers of blood may have to flow before we gain our freedom," Gandhi said. "But it must be our blood." We will win our freedom — he told them — and we will also win the respect of the British. That, he said, must be their aim. Gandhi called this "war without violence." It was successful, and helped India gain its freedom from Britain.

Now, in 1950, Martin Luther King began to wonder:

Why couldn't Gandhi's way be used by Negroes in the United States to win their freedom? Wasn't Gandhi's way also like the way of Jesus Christ? Hadn't Christ told his people to "turn the other cheek" if someone struck them? Hadn't he told them to "love your enemies"?

More and more, King began to think that Gandhi's ideas could work for Negro Americans. This idea — of fighting peacefully against evil — was called nonviolence, or nonviolent resistance. King was for nonviolence. It had worked for Gandhi. And it was moral, or right. Was nonviolence the coward's way? No, said King. It took more courage and heroism not to hit back when struck.

King was graduated from Crozer in June, 1951. He

was the top student in his class, with "A's" in all his subjects. He also won a prize of $1,200. He used this money for more study, now at Boston University.

But King wasn't an "all work and no play" man. He had many dates, and he was a smooth dancer. As for marriage, well, he thought that was for the future. Then he met Coretta Scott. She was a pretty girl who, like him, came from the South. She was in Boston studying to become a concert singer. Martin hinted on their first date that he would like her to be his wife. She wasn't interested — at first. A singing career was more important to her just then. Besides, she didn't think that preachers were very romantic. Martin soon made her change her mind about preachers. He and Coretta were married June 18, 1953. The wedding took place in the garden of her home in Marion, Alabama. The preacher who made them man and wife was Martin's father.

King and Coretta Scott were married by his father June 18, 1953.

Ebony Magazine

Rosa Parks, with E. D. Nixon (left), talks to a news reporter.

CHAPTER 4
THE JIM CROW BUSES

When Martin and Coretta moved to Montgomery, Alabama, in 1954, it was a peaceful town. But it was peaceful because hardly anyone there challenged the Jim Crow system. Some Negroes were afraid to challenge it — they might lose their jobs. Some just thought it was hopeless to fight the system. It was "peace," but it was an unjust peace, King said.

A few very brave men did speak out against Jim Crow. They were able to build a slow fire of discontent among some of Montgomery's Negroes. But so far, it was all beneath the surface.

There was one place in Montgomery where the "peace" was beginning to wear very thin. This was on the city's bus lines. There were no Negro bus drivers. Some white drivers were polite, but many were unpleasant. They often called Negro riders ugly names. Negroes paid their dimes at the front door, like everyone else. But often they were forced to get off the bus and get on again at the back door. Sometimes the buses drove off before the Negro riders had time to reach the back door.

But that wasn't all. Suppose the Negro section at the back of the bus was full. A Negro still was not allowed to sit in the white section up front even if it was empty. He had to stand in the back. There was something that bothered the Negro riders even more. Suppose the white section was full and a few more white people got on the bus. The driver could order Negroes sitting behind the white section to give up their seats and move back. Then they might have to stand. If they said "No," they were arrested. Very few ever said "No."

In March, 1955, a Negro high school girl did refuse to give up her seat to a white person. She was pulled off the bus, handcuffed, and taken to jail. This aroused Montgomery's Negroes. There was talk of boycotting the buses. A committee of Negro leaders was formed to protest. One of the leaders was King.

The group met with the manager of the bus company and the police chief. Both men were polite. They said they were very sorry about the way the girl had been treated. They would talk to the bus driver about it. And they would try to make conditions fairer for Negro bus riders.

But nothing was done. Everything went along in the same way. Negro riders were still insulted. One important thing did happen. The Negro people of Montgomery began to throw off their fear. There was a new spirit of courage and pride among them.

This new spirit burst into the open when Rosa Parks was arrested. Mrs. Parks was well known and well liked among Montgomery's Negro people. She had once been secretary of the local NAACP. Her arrest took place early Thursday evening, December 1, 1955. Soon everyone began calling everyone else on the telephone. "Have you heard the news? Rosa Parks was arrested. She wouldn't give up her seat on the bus!"

That evening a group of Negro women leaders agreed to ask for a boycott of the buses. They asked E. D. Nixon, a Pullman porter, to lead the protest. Nixon had been active in the NAACP a long time. He was one of the few men who had not been afraid to fight Jim Crow in Montgomery. He agreed to lead the boycott movement.

The next morning Nixon called King and another Negro minister, Ralph Abernathy, to tell them the news. Nixon wanted to call a meeting that night of all of Montgomery's Negro leaders to talk about the boycott. King offered his church as a meeting place. That afternoon leaflets telling about Rosa Parks' arrest and the boycott idea were handed out among Negroes.

That night the weather was warm and pleasant. More than forty Negro leaders came to the meeting in King's church. They were doctors, lawyers, teachers, businessmen, and ministers. There were union leaders and post office workers, too.

One of the ministers was chosen to lead the meeting. (Nixon had to work that night, but he was later active in the movement.) He asked for a one-day boycott of the buses as a protest. The boycott would take place on Monday, December 5. That night, there would be a big meeting, open to all. Then they would decide what to do next.

The leaders agreed to this plan. They also made plans to print more leaflets telling about the boycott. And they planned to ask the Negro taxi companies for help. They wanted Negro cabs to drive Negroes to work on Monday for a dime. That was the same price they paid on the buses.

King was full of joy when the meeting ended. He did not care that it was late at night. "The clock on the wall said it was almost midnight," King remembered, "but the clock in our souls showed that it was daybreak."

That night King was so excited he could hardly sleep. But he went to his church early next morning to see that the boycott leaflets were printed. The leaflets said:

> Another Negro has been arrested and put in jail because she refused to give up her bus seat.
>
> Don't ride the buses to work, to town, to school, or anywhere on Monday, December 5. If you work, take a cab, or share a ride, or walk.
>
> Come to a mass meeting Monday night at 7 o'clock at the Holt Street Baptist Church.

An army of women and children began handing out the leaflets that morning. Meanwhile, the Montgomery newspaper had made the boycott front page news. This was a good break for the protest movement. Practically every Negro in town knew about the boycott now. In the evening there was more good news. The Negro taxi companies had agreed to charge only ten cents to take people to and from work.

To King, the aim of the boycott was to refuse to cooperate with an evil system — Jim Crow. It reminded him of what Thoreau had written about nonviolent protest. He felt sure that this was Thoreau's way.

Sunday night King began to worry. Would the boycott work? Would the people have the courage to protest? King wasn't sure. He and Coretta agreed on this:

If three out of every five Negro riders did not use the buses on Monday, the boycott would be a success.

UPI

CHAPTER 5
THE BUS
BOYCOTT BEGINS

Both King and his wife were up early on Monday morning. They were dressed by five-thirty. There was a bus stop just a few feet from their house. The Kings could see it from their windows. The first bus was due at six o'clock. King had a cup of coffee in the kitchen while he waited. Suddenly he heard Coretta call out, "Martin, come quickly." King ran into the living room and Coretta pointed to the bus outside. "Darling," she said, "it's empty." King could hardly believe his eyes. This bus was usually filled with Negroes going to their jobs. But now it was empty! The next bus was also empty. The third bus had just two white riders.

King got into his car and drove all over town. Everywhere it was the same story — Negroes were not riding the buses. He saw only eight Negro bus riders all morning. "A miracle has taken place," King said. Montgomery's Negroes had awakened at last. Instead of using the buses, they were walking, taking cabs, or driving their cars. Some were riding on mules, and some rode on wagons pulled by horses. King was full of pride for his people. There was nothing more wonderful, he thought, than the courage of people willing to suffer for their freedom.

King then drove over to the courthouse to watch

This Montgomery bus was completely empty during Negro boycott.

Rosa Parks' trial. The judge found her guilty of breaking the bus segregation law and fined her fourteen dollars.

That afternoon the Negro leaders held another meeting. They decided to form an organization to head the protest movement. It was called the Montgomery Improvement Association (MIA). Then King was taken by surprise. Before he could say "No," he was elected president of the MIA. He really didn't want the job. Just three weeks before he had refused to run for president of the local NAACP. He felt he needed more time for his church work. But now he couldn't refuse — it was too late. So Martin Luther King became the leader of the Negro protest movement in Montgomery. It was the beginning of his career as a civil rights leader.

The Negro leaders were not sure of what to do next. Some thought it might be a good idea to call off the boycott that night. It might work one day, they said, but after that it would probably fizzle out. Then the white people would laugh at them. Finally it was agreed to let the people at the big meeting that night decide. If a lot of people came to the meeting, and they wanted the boycott to go on, then it would.

King went home to prepare the speech he would

make that night. But first he had to tell Coretta that he had been elected president of the MIA. He wondered how she would take it. She knew it would mean that he would have less time to be with her. And the job might be dangerous, because some whites might attack King. But she said, "Whatever you do, you have my backing."

King then started preparing his speech. It was already late, and he had less than half an hour to work on it. It usually took him fifteen hours to prepare his regular Sunday sermon. And this speech would be the most important of his life. King prayed for God to guide him. His main problem was this:

He wanted the speech to be strong so it would arouse his people to action;

But he did not want it to stir up hate that might lead to violence;

He had to balance action with love.

King outlined the speech in his mind. Then, skipping supper, he drove to the Holt Street Church meeting. Five blocks from the church, King ran into a traffic jam. He did not understand, at first, that all those cars were also headed for the meeting. Finally he parked his car and walked the rest of the way. The area was jammed with people. Three or four thousand were standing outside the church, unable to find room inside. (They would hear the speeches over loudspeakers.) It took King fifteen minutes to push his way to the front of the church. The excitement the crowd created, King said, was like a tidal wave.

The meeting began with the hymn, "Onward Christian Soldiers." The roar of the people's voices sounded to King "like the glad echo of Heaven itself." Soon after, King got up to speak.

He talked about the bad treatment Negroes got on

the bus lines. They were sick and tired of being insulted. They wanted justice. The time had come to protest. But, he said, the protest must be guided by law and order. They must never copy the violent ways of the Ku Klux Klan. Their ideal must be love. Didn't Jesus say, "Love your enemies, bless them that curse you"? They must not end up hating their white brothers. Then King recalled something that Booker T. Washington had once said. (Washington was a well-known Negro leader around 1900.) It was, "Let no man pull you so low as to make you hate him."

When King finished, the crowd stood up and cheered. Then Rosa Parks was asked to stand up. The people cheered her to the rafters.

Finally Ralph Abernathy spoke. He proposed that the people should not ride the buses until:

1. Negroes were treated politely by the drivers.

2. Riders were seated first-come, first-served, Negroes in the back, whites in front. (This was not asking for an end to segregation. It meant only that Negroes would not have to give up their seats to white people.)

3. Negro bus drivers were hired for buses that ran mainly through Negro sections.

Abernathy then said, "All in favor, stand."

Every person in the crowd stood up. Cheers rang out from inside and outside the church. The Negro people had voted solidly not to ride the buses.

As King drove away from the meeting his heart was filled with joy. The meeting, he felt, was itself a great victory for the Negro people. They had stood up for justice with a new spirit of dignity and honor. That day, King said, was Montgomery's moment in history. The Negro people there had started a movement that would bring new hope to Negroes everywhere.

CHAPTER 6

7089

NONVIOLENCE VS. SEGREGATION

Very soon King and the other MIA leaders had to tackle some tough problems. First, a way had to be found to drive Negro workers to and from their jobs. For a while, they depended mainly on the Negro taxi companies. They were still charging only ten cents a ride. But after a few days the Police Department put an end to this cheap service. The police told the Negro taxi companies they had to charge at least forty-five cents a ride. That was the law.

Then King asked the people for cars and drivers to take the place of the taxis. More than three hundred people offered their cars and their services as drivers. Then regular pick-up stations were set up all over the city for Negro riders. Before long the car pool system was working better than the regular bus system. Some Negroes still preferred to walk. They felt they were walking to achieve progress. One woman said, "I'm not walking for myself. I'm walking for my children and my grandchildren."

There was another problem — money. Money was needed to pay for gas for the cars, for office space and workers, and for telephones. The Negro people of Montgomery gave money for these things at their meetings. But their dimes, quarters, and dollars were not enough. Luckily, the story of their protest was now front page news. Newspapers everywhere sent reporters to "cover" the bus boycott. Soon people began sending in money from all over the United States and from all over the world. Before long there was enough money to keep the protest going.

When King was arrested, he was treated like a common criminal. After he was fingerprinted, he sat for a police file picture.

But the movement needed more than just cars and money. It needed a guiding spirit, too. A white woman who was friendly to the movement supplied the answer. She wrote a letter to the Montgomery newspaper about the bus boycott. And she compared the Negro bus protest with the Gandhi movement in India. The idea caught on. Everyone was soon talking about Gandhi and nonviolence.

King and the other leaders talked more and more about Gandhi's ideas at the big weekly meetings. (King called Gandhi "the little brown saint from India.") The people were told again and again to love rather than hate. They were told to be ready to suffer violence, but never to use violence themselves. "Our aim," King said, "must never be to defeat or shame the white man. Our aim must be to win his friendship and understanding."

In a few days a meeting was set up to try to settle the bus boycott. At the meeting were the MIA leaders, city officials, and two bus company managers. King spoke for the MIA. He told the whites what the Negroes wanted:

Polite treatment; first-come, first-served seating, with Negroes sitting in the back; the hiring of some Negro bus drivers.

At first King was hopeful. One of the city officials seemed to think the seating plan would be all right. But a bus company manager kept saying it went against the segregation laws. Then he said, "Besides, the Negroes would go around boasting of a victory they had won over the white people. We will not stand for this."

King said the Negroes would not boast, but it was useless. Finally King asked the manager just what the bus company would offer the Negroes. He said the company was willing to offer them polite treatment, but nothing more.

That wasn't enough for the Negro leaders. The meeting broke up with nothing settled. King knew then that the white leaders would put up a hard fight to defend their system.

He was right. Before long, fake stories were spread about the Negro leaders. Negro workers were told that the leaders were riding around in Cadillacs; that they were just trying to make money out of the movement. Some whites tried to divide the Negro leaders. "Get rid of King and those other young upstarts," they said. "Then we'll be able to solve everything." They tried other ways to break the boycott. But none of them worked. The Negroes and their leaders stuck together.

Then the Montgomery city officials began to "get tough." The mayor went on TV and made a speech. He said he was going to stop "pussyfooting around" with the boycott. Soon the police began arresting car pool drivers for almost any reason. Other drivers were questioned about their licenses and insurance. Riders were told there was a law against "hitch-hiking." Others were warned they would be arrested as "vagrants." Some car pool drivers quit. They were afraid of losing their licenses. But King told his people not to weaken.

Finally King himself was arrested for "speeding." King was driven in a police car to the city jail. Along the way, King almost panicked. He thought the police were driving him out of the way. Were they taking him to a lonely spot to turn him over to a lynch mob? King actually felt glad when he finally saw the jail.

But not for long. King was a leading citizen, and he had never been arrested before. But now he was treated like an ordinary criminal. First he was fingerprinted. Then he was thrown into a filthy, smelly cell with drunks and thieves. King was shocked by the terrible conditions he saw there. He promised himself that some day he would try to do something about them.

King didn't stay in jail long. The news of his arrest spread quickly all over town. His friends began rushing to the jail. Soon there was a big crowd in front of it. Now King's jailers panicked. They quickly let him out on bail. (By paying bail money, a person can go free until he has a trial.) When King saw all his friends his courage came back strong. He knew he was not alone.

"Getting tough" had failed to break the boycott. Now some white racists began to use even sneakier ways. King's home phone began to ring constantly, day and night. The callers told King (or Coretta) to "get out of town — or else." Often they called the Kings ugly names. The Kings also got many cards and letters warning them to leave town. Almost every day King was told that white men were planning to get rid of him. For the first time King realized he was in great danger. One night he told the weekly meeting of Negroes:

"If one day you find me sprawled out dead, I do not want you to strike back with a single act of violence. I want you to continue protesting with the same dignity you have shown so far."

A hush came over the audience when it heard these words.

At first, King was able to stand the ugly phone calls and letters. But after a while they began to get on his nerves. One night King felt he could take no more. He was afraid and ready to give up. He began to pray. "I am at the end of my powers," he said. "I have nothing left. I've come to the point where I can't face it alone."

At that moment, King seemed to feel the presence

of God. He heard an "inner voice" say, "Stand up for what is right, stand up for the truth, and God will be at your side forever." Almost at once, King began to lose his fear. He was ready to face anything now.

King needed all his courage very soon. Three nights later someone threw a bomb on the porch of his home. There was a big explosion. It smashed the front of the house. King was away at a meeting when it happened. But his wife and their baby daughter, "Yoki," were at home. So was a woman friend. Fortunately, no one was hurt. "Yoki" was safe asleep in a back room. Coretta and her friend ran to the back of the house when they heard "something" fall on the porch. That saved them from getting hurt, or even killed.

As soon as he heard the news King rushed back home. He found a large crowd of Negroes in front of his house. They were angry about the bombing. Many of them had guns, knives, and bottles. Police tried to break up the crowd, but couldn't. It was starting to get out of hand.

King ran inside to see if his wife and baby were safe. He was able to breathe again when he saw that they were. The mayor, police chief, and several white reporters were there. They were plainly worried about the angry crowd outside. Finally King walked out to the porch to talk to the people. He told them that he and his family were all right. Then he said, "Now let's not become panicky. If you have weapons, take them home. We cannot solve this problem through violence. Remember the words of Jesus: 'He who lives by the sword will perish by the sword.' We must love our white brothers, no matter what they do to us. Remember, if I am stopped, this movement will not stop, because God is with the movement."

There were shouts of "Amen" and "God bless you, Reverend," from the crowd. Many people were crying. Silently they went home. A bloody race riot was avoided. Soon after, the Kings began getting friendly phone calls and letters from white people in Montgomery. Usually they said, "We are with you one hundred per cent."

Meanwhile, Montgomery city officials kept looking for legal ways to break the boycott. They finally found an old state law against boycotts. Orders were then given to arrest King and more than a hundred other Negroes. King was out of town at the time. But he hurried back to Montgomery to give himself up. He was quite worried about the movement now. Would these arrests end it? Would the people now give up?

King got his answer when he drove up in front of the jail. There was a holiday spirit there. Negroes were coming from all over town *hoping* they would be arrested. Many were unhappy when they were told their names were not on the list. King was again full of pride for his people. Once they had been afraid to be arrested. Now they wanted to be arrested for the cause of freedom. King walked into the jail with firm steps. He was "booked," and then freed on bail until his trial.

The trial began on March 19. The courtroom was filled with King's friends, ministers, and newspaper reporters. Hundreds of Negroes stood outside the court. Many Negroes took the stand to defend King. Without fear, they told about the bad treatment they had gotten on the buses.

After four days, the judge found King guilty of breaking the law. He ordered King to pay a fine of five hundred dollars or go to jail for three hundred eighty-six days. This was the lightest sentence he could give King. He was "going easy," he said, because King had prevented violence. King's lawyers said they would take the case to a higher court. Meanwhile, King was freed on bail.

Many people in the court cried when King was found guilty. But King walked out of the courtroom with a smile. "I was proud of my crime," he said later. "It was the crime of joining my people in a nonviolent protest against injustice."

Wide World

Outside Montgomery courthouse, King was cheered by Coretta and many others. He had just been found guilty of leading a boycott.

CHAPTER 7
VICTORY:
INTEGRATED BUSES

The trial did not stop the protest movement. It united the Negro people more than ever. King was sure now that the protest could not be stopped. The white leaders were not dealing anymore with a scared people. They were dealing now with the "new Negro," one who had been freed from fear.

The MIA leaders now took an even bolder stand. They decided to attack bus segregation completely. Their lawyers went to a United States Federal Court. They asked the judges to end bus segregation in Alabama. They said it was against the U.S. Constitution. In May, 1954, the Supreme Court had said that school segregation was unconstitutional. It ordered schools to be desegregated. Now, in May, 1956, the MIA lawyers were hoping they could strike down bus segregation. The federal judges ruled 2-1 in favor of the MIA lawyers. They said that Alabama's bus segregation laws were unconstitutional. Montgomery city lawyers said they would take the case to the Supreme Court to argue that bus segregation was lawful. Meanwhile, the bus boycott would go on. But at last the Negroes had hope of victory.

Victory did not come easily. The city officials almost did defeat the boycott. In October they asked a Montgomery court to stop the MIA car pool. The pool, they said, was an "unlawful business."

King was sunk in gloom. He was sure that the Montgomery court would order an end to the car pool. How could the boycott go on without the cars?

King rides the first integrated bus in Montgomery. With him are Ralph Abernathy (in front) and Glenn Smiley, a white minister.

It would be almost hopeless. It was, King said, "our darkest hour."

On November 13 King and MIA lawyers were in court to defend the car pool. Around noon there was an unusual amount of noise in the courtroom. Newspaper reporters were running in and out. They seemed very excited. Suddenly one of them handed King a piece of paper. "This is what you have been waiting for," he said. "Read this."

Ku Klux Klan members burn torches at a night meeting. The KKK did not scare Montgomery Negroes after they won bus victory.

King read that the U.S. Supreme Court had agreed that Alabama's bus segregation laws were unconstitutional. His heart pounded with joy. He rushed around the courtroom, spreading the happy news. The Negroes in court shared his joy. "God Almighty has spoken from Washington, D.C.," one of them said.

Later that day the Montgomery court judge ordered an end to the car pool. But it no longer mattered. In a few days the Supreme Court order would reach Montgomery. Then bus segregation would became a thing of the past.

That night thousands of Negro people met to cheer the victory. They were in high spirits as they sang a hymn. Then Robert Graetz, a white minister, read from the Bible:

> When I was a child, I spoke as a child. I understood as a child. I thought as a child. But when I became a man, I put away childish things.

The people shouted, cheered, and waved their handkerchiefs. They knew they had "grown up." And

King knew that nonviolence had won its way into their hearts.

The meeting voted to call off the protest, but not to ride the buses until the Supreme Court order arrived.

Later that night the Ku Klux Klan rode. Forty cars full of hooded Klansmen drove through the Negro section of town. In the past, the Negroes would probably have gone inside their homes, locked the doors, and turned off the lights. Not this time. They sat on their porches with the lights on. Some even waved at the Klansmen. The KKK couldn't believe it. They quit in disgust after riding a few blocks.

Now King had another job. He had to prepare the Negro people for integrated buses. He and other leaders told the people to be polite and friendly to white riders. Above all, they must not boast of "victory over the white man." It was not a victory over the white man, King said. It was a victory for justice, for all Montgomery, and the South.

On December 20, 1956, the Supreme Court order arrived in Montgomery. Bus segregation was now over.

A bomb smashed the home of Rev. Ralph Abernathy soon after bus integration. White racists wrecked other homes and churches.

King decided to ride the first integrated bus the next morning. At 5:55 King and three of his helpers walked toward the bus stop near his home. TV cameras were covering the event and reporters were firing questions. Soon the bus arrived. The door opened and King stepped inside. The bus driver was smiling as King put his dime in the box.

"I believe you are Reverend King, aren't you?" the driver asked.

"Yes I am," King answered.

"We are glad to have you this morning," the driver said.

So the first bus was integrated in Montgomery, Alabama. It was three hundred eighty-two days after the "one-day" boycott of December 5, 1955. At first there were few problems on the buses. Most whites took the bus integration calmly. Some whites purposely sat next to Negroes to show their friendship.

But the racists in Montgomery hadn't given up yet. A few days later a wave of violence began. Buses were fired on by snipers, especially at night. On January 9 Ralph Abernathy's home and church were bombed. Robert Graetz's home was also bombed. Three other churches were hit by bombs. All the buildings were badly damaged or wrecked. On January 28 a bomb was thrown on King's porch, but it did not explode.

These acts of violence had their effect on King. He began to feel guilty. Was he the cause of them all? At a big meeting he broke down. "Lord," he said, "I hope no one will have to die as a result of our struggle for freedom in Montgomery. But if anyone has to die, let it be me."

Shouts of "No, No," came from the audience. King could not go on. Later many Negroes told him that they were all in this thing together. Only then did King feel better.

The bombers had hoped to stir up race riots. But the Negroes did not riot. King told them, "We must not return violence under any conditions. This is the way of Christ. It is the way of the cross."

Meanwhile, most white people in Montgomery were upset over the violence. Many of them did not like integration, but they believed in obeying the law. The city then arrested seven men for the bombings of the churches and homes. After that the bus integration went smoothly. King said, "The skies did not fall when integrated buses finally traveled the streets of Montgomery."

For King the Montgomery struggle had an important meaning. It showed that the Negro was now ready to struggle and suffer until he won justice.

CHAPTER 8
THE "MODERN MOSES"

May, 1957: In Washington, D.C., King demands vote for Negroes.

Ebony Magazine

When the Montgomery protest ended, King was only twenty-seven years old. Yet he already stood high in the world. He was written about in newspapers and magazines. He was called "a modern Moses." Some people said he was "the greatest Negro leader since Booker T. Washington." He was asked to speak at many meetings and dinners. He was given many honors. He was offered many jobs.

All these things might have gone to his head. But they didn't. King said, "I'm worried to death. A man who hits the peak at twenty-seven has a tough job ahead. People will expect me to pull rabbits out of the hat for the rest of my life."

King did not take any of the jobs that were offered to him. He decided to stay as pastor of his church in Montgomery. But the fight for justice would go on. Near the end of the Montgomery protest, Southern Negro leaders had formed a new organization. It was called the Southern Christian Leadership Conference (SCLC). King was elected its president. Its aim was to fight for Negro dignity everywhere. Its "weapon" was "Christian love," or nonviolence.

SCLC led other bus boycotts in the South. It also led drives to register Negroes so they could vote. At this time most Negroes in the South were kept from voting. When they tried to register, they were hindered in many ways. Usually they were given very hard "literacy" tests. Probably no one could pass these tests.

In May, 1957, King helped organize a Prayer Pilgrimage (march) to Washington, D.C. About thirty-five thousand people from thirty states met at the Lincoln Memorial. When King got up to speak, the crowd stood and cheered. King demanded that Negroes be allowed to vote.

"Give us the ballot," he said, "and we will no longer plead. We will write the proper laws. Give us the ballot and we will fill the legislatures with men of goodwill. Give us the ballot and we will get the people judges who love mercy."

For the next three years King fought hard for the Negroes' right to vote. He tried to get the United States government to support the Negroes' struggle. He traveled everywhere, making speeches for Negro rights. He was not unhappy when he was arrested. "I am happy to suffer a little," he told a group of Negro people. "It makes me feel closer to you." He was unhappy only that he had so little time now to spend with Coretta and his growing family.

Being before the public constantly also had its dangers. One day in September, 1958, King was in a department store in Harlem, a large Negro section of New York City. He was signing copies of his book, *Stride Toward Freedom*. Suddenly a Negro woman stabbed him in the chest with a letter opener. Later she was sent to a hospital for the insane. A three-hour

Getting well after stabbing, King poses with mother and Coretta.

operation saved King's life. King's doctor said, "If he had sneezed or coughed after the stabbing, the weapon would have killed him."

Near the end of 1959 King told the members of his Montgomery church that he would soon have to leave them. He was going to return to his home in Atlanta for good. He said that he had to lighten the load of his work. He had taken on too many jobs and would soon be a "wreck." In Atlanta, his father could help him with many of his church duties. Then he would be better able to carry on the struggle for civil rights.

"History," he said, "has thrust something on me which I cannot turn away."

When he finished speaking, King broke down and cried.

King returned to his father's church early in 1960. Just at this time the civil rights movement began to pick up speed. In February Negro and white students staged the first "sit-ins" at lunch counters in the South. They would sit down together at "white" lunch counters and demand service — or they would not leave. The sit-ins spread like wildfire. Soon there were sit-ins at department stores, supermarkets, libraries, and theaters. Many students were arrested and put in jail.

Martin Luther King did not start the sit-ins. They started without anyone's help, at first. The students were angry at the slow rate of desegregation in the South. They decided to do something about it themselves. But these students had learned the "ABC's" of protesting from Martin Luther King. They, too, believed in nonviolence. When they were cursed or even beaten, they did not curse or strike back. King was behind all their thoughts and feelings.

Before long King was taking an active part in the sit-ins. In October, 1960, King was arrested at a department store sit-in in Atlanta. A tough judge said King had to go to prison for four months. The next day King was thrown into jail. He was not allowed to see anyone.

The news quickly spread all over the world. At the time John F. Kennedy was running for President of the United States. He picked up his telephone and called Coretta King in Atlanta. Coretta later told about their phone talk. "He said this must be hard on me. He wanted me to know that he was thinking about us. He would do all he could to help."

Ebony Magazine

King and Coretta watch their daughter, "Yoki," play with hula hoop in 1957. King holds their son, Martin III, in his arms.

These young students are holding a sit-in at a "white" lunch counter in Little Rock, Arkansas. Counter was later integrated.

Kennedy's brother, Robert, also made a phone call. He called the judge who had sent King to jail. He wanted to know if King didn't have a right to bail. The next day, the judge agreed King did have a right to bail. King was quickly let out of jail. King said he was "deeply grateful" to John F. Kennedy. In November, 1960, most Negroes voted for Kennedy. Their votes helped to elect him President.

In 1961 Negro and white students began taking part

in "Freedom Rides." They rode buses in the South. At bus stations they used lunch counters, waiting rooms, and rest rooms that were for "whites" only. Many of them were put in jail. In jail they sang freedom songs. Their favorite freedom song was "We Shall Overcome."[1] Some of the words were:

> We'll walk hand in hand, we'll walk hand in hand,
> We'll walk hand in hand some day,
> Oh, deep in my heart I do believe
> We shall overcome some day.
> We are not afraid, we are not afraid,
> We are not afraid today.
> Oh, deep in my heart I do believe
> We shall overcome some day.

Freedom riders were sometimes beaten by white mobs. One night some freedom riders were listening to a speech by King in an Alabama church. An angry crowd of whites gathered outside the church. They tried to break in, but were stopped by United States marshals with tear gas. Finally national guardsmen had to be called in. They broke up the mob and protected King and the freedom riders.

Later King told a group of freedom riders that they "must develop the quiet courage of dying for a cause. We would not like to see anyone die. We all love life and there are no martyrs here. But we are all aware that we may have some deaths."

---

[1] WE SHALL OVERCOME
New Words and Music arrangement by Zilphia Horton, Frank Hamilton, Guy Carawan and Pete Seeger TRO © Copyright 1960 and 1963, Ludlow Music, Inc. New York, New York. Royalties derived from this composition are being contributed to The Freedom Movement under the trusteeship of the writers.

CHAPTER 9
THE BATTLE
OF BIRMINGHAM

In the spring and summer of 1962 King had his first great setback. He and his helpers tried to end segregation in the town of Albany, Georgia. Negroes there took part in marches, sit-ins, and prayed in the streets. The Albany police chief was tough. He did not use violence, but he jailed the Negroes constantly for breaking local laws. He arrested King three times. Finally the protest fizzled out.

Many people then said that King and nonviolence were "washed up." King felt only that he had made some mistakes in Albany, and that he had learned from them. King now wanted more than ever to prove that nonviolent protest *did* work. He looked about for a city that would be the right place to prove it. What was the toughest Jim Crow city in the South? King had no doubt that it was Birmingham, Alabama. Birmingham had refused to obey the Supreme Court's school desegregation order. One city official had said

Eugene "Bull" Connor (front), Birmingham police chief, said he would keep Negroes "in their place." He arrested many of them.

that "blood would flow in the streets first." Almost everything was still segregated in Birmingham. Even the water fountains were marked "colored" or "white." A United States Senator had been arrested there for walking through a door marked "colored." Birmingham's police chief, Eugene "Bull" Connor, boasted that he knew how to keep Negroes "in their place." Worst of all, violence and brutality against Negroes were commonplace. In the past six years, seventeen Negro churches and homes had been bombed.

Most Negro people in Birmingham were afraid to speak out against Jim Crow. So were many white citizens who disliked the system. King felt that Birmingham was the place to strike at Jim Crow. If some public places in Birmingham could be desegregated, it would be a big defeat for Jim Crow everywhere.

King and his SCLC helpers carefully drew up a "battle" plan. They did not want to repeat any of the mistakes they had made in Albany, Georgia. The plan was called "Project C." The Negro leaders decided to take direct aim at Birmingham's Jim Crow stores and eating places. Negroes would boycott downtown stores with Jim Crow lunch counters and washrooms. They would also hold sit-ins, kneel-ins, and marches. They would start slowly, then step up the protest day by day.

On Wednesday, April 3, 1963, the protest began quietly with a few sit-ins at Jim Crow lunch counters. The "sit-inners" were asked to leave and refused. They were then arrested and put in jail. Police chief Bull Connor didn't think much of the protest — then.

That night the first of many big meetings was held by the SCLC. The people sang freedom songs. Many wanted to take an active part in the protests. They were then trained in the ways of nonviolence. They would watch plays in which "white policemen" beat "protesters." The "protesters" did not strike back. That was the lesson they had to learn.

On Saturday, April 6, there was an orderly protest march on City Hall. The marchers were stopped by police. Bull Connor ordered the Negroes to "break it up." They refused. Many were arrested. Negroes watching on the sidewalk cheered them and clapped their hands. The marchers went off to jail singing freedom songs. "Something was happening to the Negroes in this city," King thought. "Something was taking place in the mind, heart, and soul of Negroes all over America."

The protests grew larger every day. The jails began to fill up. So far, Bull Connor had also used nonviolence. His police, in fact, had been most polite as they arrested Negroes. Then, on April 10, the city got a court order to stop the protest movement. King decided he would not obey the order, something he had never done before. He felt he had no choice. The order, if obeyed, could break the back of his movement. It was, he said, his duty not to obey it. He did it because he felt the law was wrong in this case, since it led to injustice.

King planned to hold another march and let himself be arrested. But he soon got some very bad news. The city had cut off the protesters' supply of bail money in Birmingham. Without bail, many protesters might have to stay in jail a long time. King, too, would be "stuck" behind bars. King's helpers begged him not to go to jail. The movement needed a lot of money now, and King was the only man who could get it. "If you go to jail," one Negro leader said, "the battle of Birmingham is lost."

CHAPTER 10
BIRMINGHAM: KING GOES TO JAIL AND WINS

King didn't know what to do. He had told his people they should go to jail cheerfully when fighting injustice. What would they say about him if he didn't go to jail? Yet King didn't want to see his movement wrecked. That might happen if he did go to jail.

King had a feeling of doom. Then he started to think about "twenty million black people who dreamed that some day they might find their way to the promised land of integration and freedom." Suddenly, King had no more doubts about what to do. He put on blue denim work clothes. Then he told his helpers he would go to jail.

UPI
This picture of Martin Luther King in a Birmingham jail was taken in 1967. King first went to jail in that city in 1963.

"I don't know what will happen," he said. "I don't know where the bail money will come from. But I have to make an act of faith."

King asked Ralph Abernathy to join him, and Abernathy agreed. The next day they led a group of fifty marchers downtown. Negroes lined the streets. They were smiling and joined the marchers in singing. Then Bull Connor ordered his men to arrest the marchers and take them to jail. In jail, King was put in "solitary" — no one was allowed to visit him. His cell was narrow and dark. Light came in through a window near the top of his cell in the morning, but that was all. King was sunk in gloom. He felt that his whole movement was in great danger. Everything seemed to be going dark. He could not see the light anywhere.

Coretta had not gone with King to Birmingham. She had just given birth to their fourth child, and had to stay home in Atlanta. Now she was terribly worried about her husband. She had not had a single telephone call from him in two days. Finally she decided she had to do something. She remembered how John F. Kennedy had called her in October, 1960. This time she called President Kennedy in Washington. President Kennedy was away in Florida. But she was able to speak to his brother, Attorney General Robert Kennedy. She said she was afraid her husband was not safe. He said he would do everything he could to help King.

Later Coretta's phone rang. Her two-year-old son, Dexter, picked up the telephone. Coretta heard the operator say that the President of the United States was calling from Florida. Would she please get her son off the phone? Coretta finally got Dexter to let go of the phone. Then she heard the President's voice. "How are you, Mrs. King?" he asked. Then he told her he would look into her husband's trouble right away.

Both the President and his brother called Birmingham. Conditions improved for King almost immediately. He was allowed to call Coretta. And he was allowed a visit from his lawyer. His lawyer had good news. A lot of bail money had been raised by friends. King would soon be able to go free. Later King said, "I knew then I had never been truly in solitary. God's companionship doesn't stop at the door of a jail cell. I didn't know whether the sun was shining or not at that moment. But I knew that once again I could see the light."

While King was in jail, he wrote a letter that is now famous. This "Letter from a Birmingham Jail" was written to answer a group of white ministers. These ministers had found fault with King for many reasons.

1. They said that King was an "outsider" in Birmingham.

King said he was in Birmingham to fight for justice. No one is an outsider in such a fight.

2. They said his protest was "untimely." He should have waited to give the new mayor a chance to improve conditions.

King said that, for Negroes, "wait" usually meant "never." He said that the Negro people had already waited much too long for their rights. They could not wait any longer.

3. They said that King should not have used sit-ins and marches. He should have had talks with the city officials.

King said that the aim of the sit-ins and marches was to bring about talks. In this case, it was the *only* way to open the door to talks.

4. They said that King was breaking the law.

King said there were two kinds of laws. There were just laws and unjust laws. A person has a duty to obey just laws. He also has a duty not to obey unjust laws. Segregation laws, he said, were unjust laws.

5. They said that King's nonviolent ways were "extreme" — went too far.

King said that nonviolence was not extreme. Some Negroes, he said, wanted to do nothing about ending segregation. Other Negroes were full of hatred and might use violence against whites. These were the "black nationalists." The nonviolent movement stood in between those two groups. King warned that whites must support the nonviolent movement. Otherwise, millions of Negroes might turn to black nationalism. That, he said, would lead to a "racial nightmare."

After eight days, King and Abernathy left jail. Now King took another bold step. He invited high school and college students to take part in the protests. He needed their help. And he felt young people should have their own stake in freedom.

The teenagers were eager to join the protest movement. They joined by the hundreds and were trained in nonviolence. On May 2, more than a thousand teenagers marched — and went to jail. For the first time King was able to do what Gandhi had said: "Fill up the jails." At one school the principal locked the gates to keep the students in. The students climbed over the gates and joined the marchers. They sang as they marched and as they were taken to jail. Now the young people were fighting for freedom, too.

Bull Connor decided it was time to "get tough." The

next day police used their clubs on the marchers. Police dogs were turned on them, tearing their clothes and flesh. Streams of water from fire hoses knocked them to the ground. Pictures of this violence were shown in newspapers all over the country. People were shocked. Many began to support the Negro protesters. They sent money to their movement in Birmingham. And in Birmingham itself some white people also began to boycott the downtown stores.

Bull Connor's men were soon shaken by the protesters. One day hundreds of Negroes began a march on the city jail. Connor ordered them to turn back. The Negroes politely said "No."

Then Connor ordered his men to turn on the powerful fire hoses. But the marchers were not afraid. Slowly they began to move forward. The police couldn't believe it. They fell back, without turning on the hoses. The Negroes marched past them, unharmed, to the jail. It was, King said, "fantastic."

By this time, Birmingham's business leaders were beginning to weaken. They started to hold secret meetings with the Negro leaders to end the protest. The Negro leaders wanted:

1. The desegregation of lunch counters, rest rooms, and drinking fountains in stores;

2. More jobs, and better jobs, for Negroes;

3. The release of all protesters still in jail;

4. A group of Negroes and whites to work out a plan for desegregating Birmingham even further.

On May 7 a large group of Birmingham businessmen met to talk over these demands. Most of the businessmen were against them. They broke up the meeting to go to lunch. When they got to the street they could hardly believe what they saw. Thousands

Powerful fire hoses were turned on some marchers in Birmingham and trained police dogs tore the clothes and flesh of protesters.

of Negroes had marched into the downtown section. The jails were so full the police couldn't arrest them. The Negroes crowded the sidewalks and streets. They sat on the floors of the downtown stores. They were peaceful, and they were singing freedom songs. The businessmen realized the protest movement could not be stopped. One white businessman said, "I've been thinking this thing through. We ought to be able to work something out."

The end came three days later. The Negroes won almost all their demands. Reporters flashed the news all over the world. It made big headlines in the United States.

But their troubles weren't over yet. Some white people were boiling mad over the peace agreement. The next night, the Ku Klux Klan held a meeting. Soon after, the home of King's brother, Reverend A. D. King, was bombed. So was the Gaston Motel, where King was staying while in Birmingham. Neither one of the Kings was injured. Martin Luther King was spending that night at home in Atlanta.

The bombings aroused many Birmingham Negroes. Some, who were not part of King's movement, fought with the police. There was a riot. This was just what the white racists wanted. They hoped to upset the peace agreement. But President Kennedy quickly ordered three thousand soldiers to Birmingham. And King rushed back to calm his people. These actions stopped the troublemakers and brought back peace.

Birmingham was another great victory for King and the Negro people. The peace agreement did not mean that segregation would end in Birmingham overnight. Some people would still fight for it and use violence. But Birmingham had taken a great step toward equality for its citizens. And Jim Crow, King felt, was now on its deathbed.

CHAPTER 11
AFTER BIRMINGHAM:
THE NEGRO REVOLUTION

The victory in Birmingham had its effect on Negroes everywhere. In the summer of 1963 they rose up in hundreds of American cities to demand "Freedom now!" They were tired of suffering silently and waiting patiently. It was now a hundred years after the Emancipation Proclamation had freed the slaves. But were Negroes really free? Not while they were still segregated. Not while they couldn't vote. Not while they couldn't get good jobs. They were angry now. They marched in the streets and staged sit-ins in government buildings. They stopped traffic and picketed stores. There were Negro protests everywhere, every day. King called the summer of 1963 the beginning of the Negro Revolution. And no one doubted that Martin Luther King was the leader of that revolution.

The Negro protests that summer were felt by all Americans. In the White House, President Kennedy said,

Are we to say to the world that
• this is the land of the free, except for Negroes?
• we have no second-class citizens, except for Negroes?
• we have no ghettos, except for Negroes?

Soon after, President Kennedy asked Congress for a strong civil rights bill to do away with segregation. But the protests were already getting results. Thousands of schools, parks, hotels, and lunch counters were integrated. Many companies began to hire Negroes for the first time. Many began to offer Negroes important jobs for the first time. Many began to promote Negroes they already had.

But the biggest change was in the Negroes them-

Summer, 1963: New York Negroes, chained together, stage protest.

selves. They had a new pride in their race. One white businessman asked, "Am I just imagining it, or are the Negroes I see around town walking a little taller these days?"

The events of 1963 reached their peak in the famous March on Washington. The idea of the march was to demand "Jobs and Freedom." The idea caught on rapidly. On August 28, 1963, about two hundred and fifty thousand Americans arrived in Washington, D.C. They came from almost every state in the Union. They came in buses and cars, trains and airplanes.

UPI
Summer, 1963: Police in Nashville, Tennessee, push back youths.

They were Negro and white, old and young. They were of every religion, every class, every profession, every party. In the morning they marched peacefully to the Lincoln Memorial, singing along the way. Then this "army without guns" listened to speeches by many civil rights leaders. But the one they had really come to see and hear was Martin Luther King. And King did not let them down. The speech he made that day will be remembered for a long time.

Summer, 1963: This civil rights rally took place in Chicago.

"I have a dream," he said. "It is a dream deeply rooted in the American Dream. I have a dream that one day this nation will rise up and live out the true meaning of its creed; 'We hold these truths to be self-evident, that all men are created equal.'

"I have a dream that one day on the red hills of Georgia sons of former slaves and sons of former slaveowners will be able to sit down together at the table of brotherhood. I have a dream that one day

67

John F. Kennedy and King joke before JFK was elected President. As the President, Kennedy asked for a strong civil rights bill.

even the state of Mississippi, a state sweltering with the heat of injustice, sweltering with the heat of oppression, will be transformed into an oasis of freedom and justice.

"I have a dream that one day my four little children will live in a nation where they will not be judged by the color of their skin but by the content of their character.

"I have a dream that one day every valley shall be exalted, every hill and mountain shall be made low. The rough places will be made plain, and the crooked places will be made straight. This is the faith that I go back to the South with. With this faith we shall be able to hew out of the mountain of despair a stone of hope. With this faith we will be able to work together, to pray together, to struggle together, to go to jail together, to stand up for freedom together, knowing we will be free one day.

Martin Luther King makes his famous "I have a dream" speech in Washington, D.C.

"This will be the day when all of God's children will be able to sing with new meaning, 'let freedom ring.' So let freedom ring from the prodigious hilltops of New Hampshire. Let freedom ring from the mighty mountains of New York. But not only that. Let freedom ring from Stone Mountain of Georgia. Let freedom ring from every hill and molehill of Mississippi, from every mountainside.

"When we allow freedom to ring — when we let it ring from every city and every hamlet, from every state and every city, we will be able to speed up that day when all of God's children, black men and white men, Jews and Gentiles, Protestants and Catholics, will be able to join hands and sing in the words of the old Negro spiritual,

'Free at last, Free at last, Great God amighty,
We are free at last.' "

Wide World

UPI

At left: The great crowd that met at the Lincoln Memorial to hear King and other speakers, August 28, 1963. At right: King and other civil rights leaders head the March on Washington earlier in the day.

71

When King finished, many men and women in the crowd were crying.

Millions of Americans watched the March and heard King's speech on television. They knew that day they were watching a rare moment in history.

That summer, Negroes moved forward faster than at any time since the Civil War period. But their victories did not mean that white racists had given up their fight. There were still many acts of violence against Negroes. Two were especially shocking:

On June 12, 1963, Medgar Evers, a well-known Negro civil rights leader, was shot and killed in Jackson, Mississippi.

On September 15, 1963, a bomb was thrown into a Baptist Church in Birmingham, Alabama. Four Negro girls in a Sunday school class were killed.

Then, on November 22, 1963, there was another act of violence that affected the whole country. A sniper's bullets snuffed out the life of President Kennedy in Dallas, Texas, that day. No one could be sure at first who killed President Kennedy. But Martin Luther King placed the blame on a "climate of hate" rather than on any one person. He said:

"We are all involved in the death of President Kennedy. We tolerated hate. We tolerated violence in all walks of life. We tolerated the idea that a man's life was sacred only if we agreed with his views. And so the plague spread until it claimed a warmly loved President. We mourned a man who had become the pride of the nation. But we grieved as well for ourselves because we knew we were sick."

In June President Kennedy had asked Congress for a strong civil rights bill to end segregation. It had not yet been passed when President Kennedy died. The new President, Lyndon B. Johnson, spoke to Congress five days later. Johnson asked Congress to pass the civil rights bill as soon as possible. He said it would be the best way to honor the memory of John F. Kennedy.

On July 2, 1964, Congress passed and President Johnson signed a strong civil rights bill. It was stronger even than the one Kennedy had asked for. Martin Luther King was present when President Johnson signed it in the White House. This bill became the Civil Rights Act of 1964. It went a long way toward making the Negro a first-class citizen. This is what it said:

• No one can be kept out of such places as hotels, lunch counters, gas stations, and theaters because of his race.

President Lyndon B. Johnson shakes hands with King after the signing of Civil Rights Act of 1964. Scene was the White House.

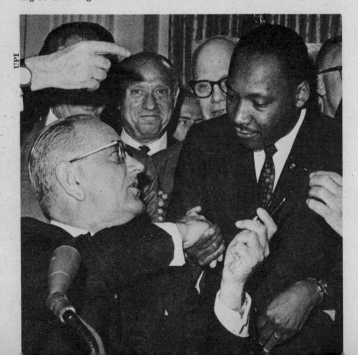

- No one can be kept out of public places such as parks, swimming pools, beaches, or libraries because of his race.

- Anyone who passed the sixth grade in school must be allowed to vote without taking a test.

- Companies with more than a hundred workers and unions with more than a hundred members may not keep out anyone who has the skill to do the work.

- The United States Attorney-General can take school officials to court in places that still have segregated schools.

By now, King's name was known all over the world. He had won many honors, both in the United States and other countries. In October, 1964, King won the highest honor of all, the Nobel Peace Prize. It is given by the Nobel Prize Committee of the Norwegian National Assembly. The award, King said, was "a sign that world opinion was on the side of those struggling for freedom and dignity." It was a tribute to the millions of people who followed nonviolent ways in seeking justice. He was sure it would give him "new courage" to carry on the fight for justice.

Later King flew to Oslo, Norway, to accept the prize. He told King Olav V of Norway and others:

"I am mindful that only yesterday in Birmingham, Alabama, our children, crying out for brotherhood, were answered with fire hoses, snarling dogs, and even death. I am mindful that only yesterday, in Philadelphia, Mississippi, young people seeking to secure the right to vote were brutalized and murdered.

"Therefore, I must ask why this prize is awarded to a movement that is beleaguered and committed to unrelenting struggle; to a movement which has not won the very peace and brotherhood which is the essence of the Nobel Prize. After contemplation, I conclude that this award which I receive on behalf of that movement is profound recognition that nonviolence is the answer to the crucial political and moral question of our time — the need for man to overcome oppression and violence without resorting to violence and oppression.

"I accept this award today with an abiding faith in America and an audacious faith in the future of mankind. I refuse to accept the idea that man is mere flotsam and jetsam in the river of life which surrounds him. I refuse to accept the view that mankind is so tragically bound to the starless midnight of racism and war that the bright daylight of peace and brotherhood can never become a reality."

King gave the Nobel Prize money — $54,000 — to the civil rights movement.

Martin Luther King gets Nobel Peace Prize from King Olav of Norway. Coretta is at the right. The date was December 10, 1964.

CHAPTER 12   1965:

The fight for justice soon took Martin Luther King to Selma, Alabama. In Alabama and other states in the South Negroes were still kept from voting. In Selma more than half the people were Negroes. But only one voter in every hundred was a Negro. Negroes who tried to register to vote in Selma were given a hard time. They might be asked to recite from memory a long state law. Sometimes they were turned away because they didn't spell out their middle names.

King calls for a protest march to Montgomery after a Negro was shot. "We must stand up for what is right," he told the crowd.

thousand Negroes were put in jail. One of them was Martin Luther King.

Then one night a Negro marcher was shot and killed in a nearby town. Before he died he said that a state trooper had done the shooting. King then called for a protest march from Selma to the State Capitol at Montgomery, fifty miles away. He said, "I can't promise you that it won't get your house bombed. I can't promise you that it won't get you beaten up. But we must stand up for what is right!"

Governor George Wallace of Alabama forbade the march. But on Sunday, March 7, about six hundred fifty Negroes and a few whites started out for Montgomery anyway. Just outside Selma, they were

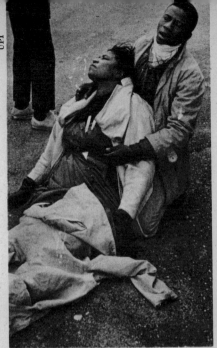

Police broke up the
first freedom march
using clubs, whips,
and tear gas (p. 81).
At right are two of
the injured marchers.

met by a solid wall of sixty Alabama state troopers.
Sheriff Clark's men were also there, some on
horseback. A state policeman ordered the marchers to
go back. He gave them two minutes to obey. The
marchers stayed where they were. Then the police
moved on the marchers. They used clubs, whips, and
tear gas on them. Some marchers fell and were kicked
by horses' hoofs. More than seventy were hurt and
had to be treated in hospitals.

Many people in the United States became very
angry. There were protest marches in many cities.
King then ordered another march for Tuesday, March
9. Now, more than four hundred white ministers,
priests, and rabbis rushed to Selma from all over the
United States. They took their place at the side of the
marchers. The second march was again turned back
by the police, this time peacefully.

But that night white hoodlums beat up three white ministers in Selma. One of the ministers, James Reeb of Boston, died. The nation was shocked. President Johnson called it "an American tragedy which cannot and will not be repeated." Many more people then went to Selma to join the marchers.

Finally a United States judge ordered Governor Wallace and others not to stop the march. He also ordered Governor Wallace to give the marchers police protection. Wallace said the state didn't have the money to protect the marchers. Then President Johnson ordered the Alabama National Guard and United States army troops to do the job.

On March 21 more than three thousand marchers started out for Montgomery. They were led by Martin Luther King and Ralph Bunche of the United Nations. The march took five days. At night the marchers slept

in fields. Hot meals were brought by trucks. On the fifth day the marchers reached the steps of the State Capitol. They were joined there by thousands of other whites and Negroes. They wanted to talk to Governor Wallace about Negro voting rights. But Wallace would not see them. Then Martin Luther King made a speech.

He said, "They told us we wouldn't get here. And some said we would get here only over their dead bodies. But all the world knows today that we are here and saying, 'We ain't goin' let nobody turn us around.' "

King called for more marches, on segregated schools, on poverty, and on voting places. "We must have our freedom now," he said. "We must have the right to vote. We must have equal protection of the law."

The marchers left peacefully. But that night, there was more violence. A white woman civil rights worker was shot and killed in her car. Three members of the Ku Klux Klan were arrested. Two of them were later sent to jail for ten years.

Before the march began President Johnson spoke to Congress. He said, "It is wrong — dead wrong — to deny any of your fellow Americans the right to vote. All of us must overcome . . . bigotry and injustice. And we *shall* overcome."

Then President Johnson asked Congress to pass a new voting rights bill. This bill became the Voting Rights Act of 1965. It did away with tests for voters in places where less than half the people had voted in 1964. It also put United States government workers in charge of registering voters in these places. It was a great victory for the Selma freedom marchers.

UPI

Thousands of Negroes and whites gather in front of the State Capitol in Montgomery, Alabama, after five-day freedom march.

Poverty in Negro ghettos led to rioting. Above,
jobless men. Below, a ghetto child.

Helen Levitt

Wide World

CHAPTER 13
THE FIGHT
AGAINST POVERTY

King stood at the peak of his career when he spoke at Selma. But already his dream of nonviolence had been shaken. In the summer of 1964 riots broke out in Negro ghettos in several northern cities. It was the first of the "long, hot summers." In the next three summers the riots got much worse. Watts, Newark, and Detroit made the biggest headlines. In these and other cities some Negroes burned homes, looted stores, and fought police and troops. The damage to some of these cities was great. The cost in human lives was also high. More than one hundred forty people were killed. More than forty-five hundred were injured.

The causes of these riots were plain. Civil rights had helped Negroes in many important ways. But

A Detroit street burns during 1967 riots (above).
Soldiers search rioters (below).

most Negroes living in the ghettos were still very poor. Many had no jobs. Those who had jobs usually did unskilled work at low pay. Life was a daily struggle to pay the landlord, the butcher, the grocer. The ghetto houses were old and rundown. Pipes leaked and walls cracked. There were rats, roaches, and bugs in many. There was sickness and hunger. And, as a result of this misery, there was dope addiction and crime. For many Negroes, there did not seem to be any way out of these dark ghettos. In despair and anger they began to burn them down.

And now there were new Negro leaders on the scene. Some of them seemed to fan the flames of riot and disorder. These men talked of "black power," not of "freedom" and "dignity." They talked of "war in the streets," not of "love" and "nonviolence." One of them said, "Violence is necessary. It is as American as cherry pie. If you give me a gun and tell me to shoot my enemy, I might just shoot Lady Bird Johnson [President Johnson's wife]. . . . If America doesn't come around, we're going to burn America down, brother."

Martin Luther King understood the causes of the ghetto riots. He had always said that segregation and poverty were "twin evils." The aim of segregation, he said, was to keep Negroes poor. In 1963 King said, "Equality means dignity. And dignity demands a job and a pay check that lasts through the week."

Until 1965 King had fought mainly for civil rights and an end to segregation. But the ghetto riots upset him deeply. More and more he began to turn his attention to the problem of poverty. King made more marches, but now they were usually for better homes, schools, and jobs for ghetto people.

In the summer of 1966 King went to Chicago to demand integrated housing and slum clearance. On August 6 he led a march of about six hundred Negroes through an all-white section. Crowds of angry whites threw stones, bottles, eggs, and cherry bombs at the marchers. King himself was hit on the head by a rock. He fell, but got up and continued the march. Later a knife was thrown at him. It missed him, but it hit a white youth in the neck. The march touched off five hours of near-rioting by thousands of whites. They were battled by more than nine hundred police. Many whites were arrested.

Other marches in Chicago were also met by whites throwing rocks and bottles. They swore at the marchers and shouted "white power." King did not give up. He called for more marches. He put on work

King's marches in Chicago for open housing angered these whites.

clothes and helped clean up a slum alley with a shovel. He also nailed a list of the Negroes' complaints to the door of City Hall.

At this time, too, King began speaking out against the war in Viet Nam. He was against it because all forms of violence saddened him. "Man," he said, "has reached the day when violence toward another human being must become as hateful as eating another's flesh. Nonviolence, the answer to the Negroes' need, may become the answer to the most desperate need of all humanity — peace." King felt strongly, too, that the war in Viet Nam was slowing down the drive for civil rights and the "war on poverty" at home.

UPI
King was knocked down by a rock during one march in Chicago.

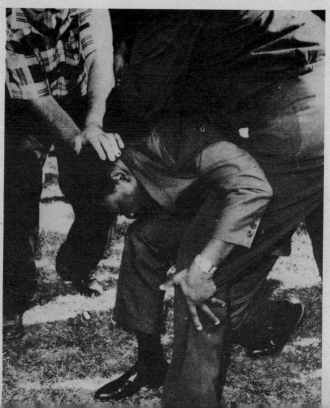

King looked worried as he led march in Memphis for striking garbage men. Soon after, a riot broke out, ending the march.

CHAPTER 14
FREE AT LAST

As 1968 began, King was planning another march on Washington. It was to be a march of poor people, Negro and white. Its aim was to get Congress to pass laws to help all poor people. He wanted "jobs or income" for everyone. This march was to take place on April 22, 1968.

But in March, King went to Memphis, Tennessee. Negro garbage workers were on strike there. King wanted to help them win a pay raise. He was going to lead a nonviolent march for them. The march was set for Thursday, March 28. Soon after it began some Negro teenagers began looting. The result was a riot that ended the march. The rioting saddened King. He felt it was bad for the cause of nonviolence. He went home to Atlanta. He did not want to go back to Memphis. But, he thought, that would mean giving up to violence. "Nonviolence is on trial in Memphis," he told friends.

So King went back to Memphis to start another march. On April 3 he made a speech there. Toward the end, he talked about death. He had been warned he would be killed in Memphis, he said. His plane from Atlanta had been searched for bombs.

"But it really doesn't matter with me now," he said. "Because I have been to the mountaintop. And I've looked over, and I've seen the promised land. I may not get there with you. But I want you to know tonight that we as a people will get to the promised land. So I'm happy tonight. I'm not worried about anything. I'm not fearing any man. Mine eyes have seen the glory of the coming of the Lord!"

It was King's last speech.

UPI

King was shot and killed on the balcony of this Memphis motel.

The next day King met with his helpers in his room. It was on the second floor of a motel. King told his helpers that nonviolence was the only hope of saving the soul of this nation. He talked about the life of Jesus and Gandhi. Then he told his helpers, "I have conquered the fear of death."

Later King went out on the balcony outside his room. He wanted to relax for a while before going to eat dinner. From the balcony King talked to two friends standing below. It was getting chilly. King's driver nagged him to put on a coat. "Okay," King said with a grin, "I will."

Suddenly there was a sound of a rifle shot. It came from a rooming house across the way. The bullet ripped into King's face and slammed him against the wall. Then King fell to the floor. Blood was pouring from a hole in his neck. He died in a Memphis hospital less than an hour later. One of his helpers said, "Murder, murder! Doc [King] said that's not the way." And one woman cried, "Oh, Lord Jesus, they didn't have to kill him. They didn't have to kill him."

King's body was brought home to Atlanta. It was placed at the altar of the Ebenezer Baptist Church, where he had been copastor with his father. Everywhere in the nation there was shock and grief. Jacqueline Kennedy, the widow of John F. Kennedy, wrote a letter to Coretta King. She asked, "When will our country learn that to live by the sword is to perish by the sword?"

On Tuesday, April 9, the funeral began. Inside the little church, along with Coretta and her children, were many famous people. Outside the church were thousands of plain people. Many words were said in honor of Martin Luther King. But the words that seemed to touch the people most were spoken by King himself. A tape recording was played of part of

King's body was taken to the cemetery on an old farm wagon (left). Mrs. King wept softly at services (right).

the last sermon King made in his church. His voice said:

"If any of you are around when I have to meet my day, I don't want a long funeral. And if you get somebody to deliver the eulogy [farewell speech], tell him not to talk too long. Tell him not to mention that I have a Nobel Peace Prize. That isn't important. Tell him not to mention that I have three hundred or four hundred other awards. That's not important.

"I'd like someone to mention that day that Martin Luther King, Jr., tried to give his life serving others. I'd like for somebody to say that Martin Luther King, Jr., tried to love somebody.

"I want you to be able to say that day that I did try to feed the hungry. I want you to be able to say that I did try in my life to clothe the naked. I want you to say on that day that I did try in my life to visit those who were in prison. And I want you to say that I tried to love and serve humanity."

Martin Luther King's coffin was placed on an old farm wagon. King had planned to use it in his poor people's march on Washington. The wagon was drawn by two Georgia mules. About a hundred thousand people slowly marched behind it.

At the cemetery, Ralph Abernathy, King's friend and helper, said, "The grave is too narrow for his soul, but we commit his body to the ground."

The gravestone had King's name, the year he was born, the year he died. Under them were a few words from a spiritual King had loved. He used these words to end his "I have a dream speech" in Washington in 1963. The words were:

"Free at last, free at last,
Thank God Almighty I'm free at last."

King was buried in this grave in Atlanta, Georgia, where he was born 39 years before. A worker touches up letters on the stone.